See Life
Coloring Book
Created By
C.M. Barth

WELCOME

LOVING
NATURE

SEE LIFE

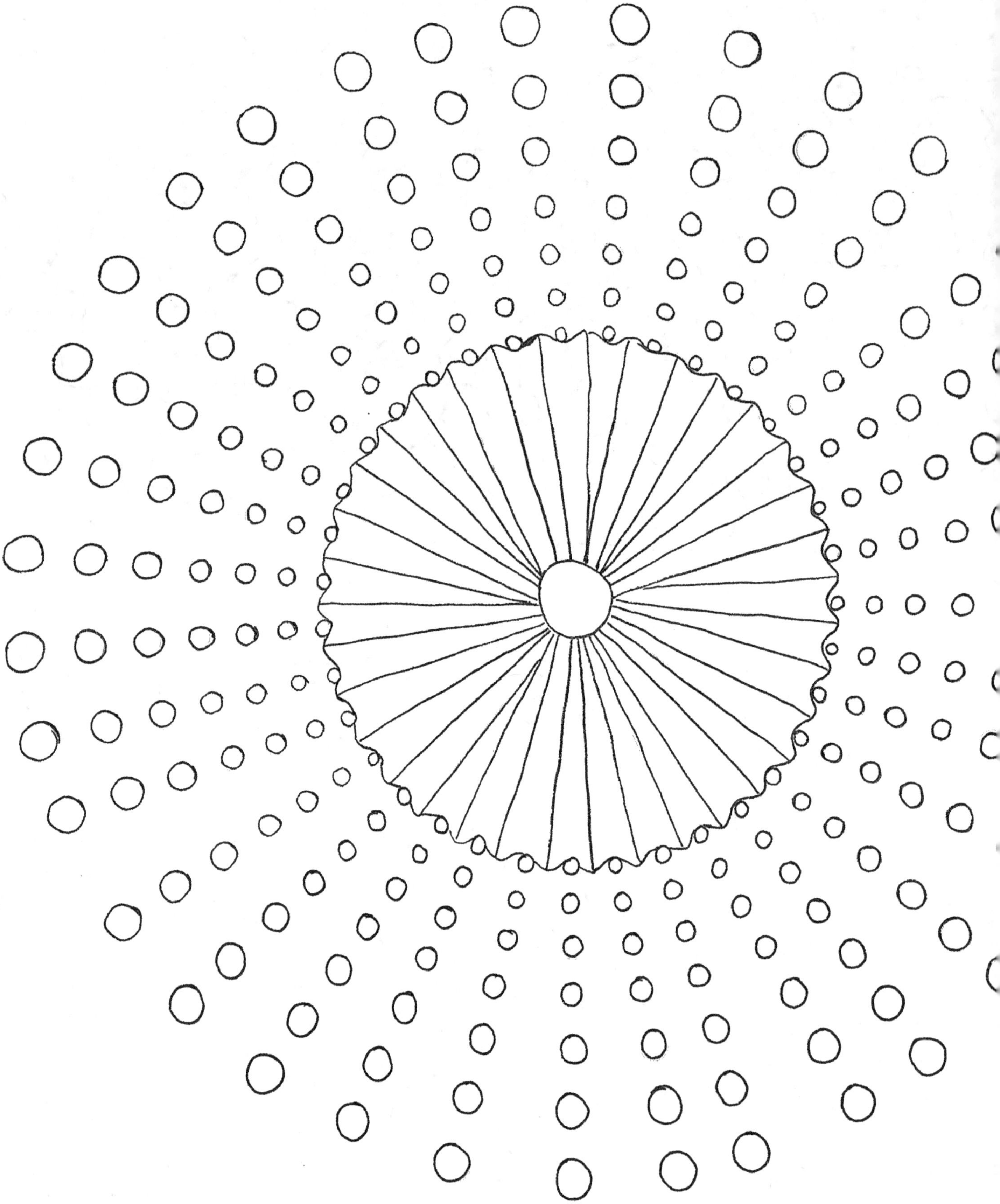

butterfly

LIFE

www.ingramcontent.com/pod-product-compliance
Lightning Source LLC
Chambersburg PA
CBHW081144280526
45787CB00007B/3225
* 9 7 8 1 5 3 3 3 1 2 9 8 3 *